# FINDING YOUR SPIRITUAL DIRECTION *as* *a* CATECHIST

## Helpful skills and reflections for personal growth

### WILLIAM B. MILLER

**TWENTY-THIRD PUBLICATIONS**
twentythirdpublications.com

TWENTY-THIRD PUBLICATIONS
One Montauk Avenue, Suite 200
New London, CT 06320
(860) 437-3012 or (800) 321-0411
www.twentythirdpublications.com

ISBN: 978-1-62785-325-5
Library of Congress Control Number: 2017945079
Printed in the U.S.A.

 A Division of Bayard, Inc.

# Contents

# Acknowledgments

*No one writes a book in a vacuum. There are always a
great number of people who offer support of one kind
or another, from prayer support to information support,
from time and energy to love and perseverance.*

*I thank the many experts who contributed information
for this book. They are authors and teachers, some of them
having lived several thousand years ago. Together they
have written the sacred Scriptures and the material that
composes the content of the deposit of our faith. The roots of
Catholicism are very deep, and for that I am most grateful!*

*I thank the many friends who have helped me understand and
appreciate my faith by spending time with me in very meaningful
relationships that have helped me shape the stories of my life.*

*I thank the people who took time to read
and comment on this manuscript.*

*I thank those who have acted as spiritual directors and spiritual
companions for me over these many years. They have been
invaluable in encouraging and empowering my spiritual growth.*

*I thank my editors at Twenty-Third Publications, Kathy
Hendricks and Dan Connors, who provided tremendous
support and encouragement for this first-time book author.*

*I thank God, especially for my loving wife, Marilyn, who has
been my number one cheerleader and support person for almost
40 years. This book could not have been written without her.*

*I dedicate this work to Marilyn, our daughter, Laura, and
to my loving parents, Orville B. and Margaret Ann Miller.
They performed their role as my "primary catechists" with
profound love and dedication. I am eternally grateful!*

# INTRODUCTION

Finding your spiritual direction as a catechist is much like finding your spiritual direction as a dentist or a nurse, a lawyer or a carpenter, a computer programmer or a plumber, a spouse, a parent, a single person, etc. While each of us is unique and the context of each of our life situations will differ from that of all other people, there are certain spiritual principles that remain the same. I don't pretend to capture them all between the covers of this work; however, I think I have a bead on some of the most important ones.

I believe that you don't have to be a catechist in the formal sense of the word in order to enjoy and benefit from this book. The principles contained herein are important for anyone who wishes to grow in love of God, neighbor, and self. And who (other than God) knows! After reading this book you may decide that you have been called to officially become a catechist. Moreover, we each have opportunities every day to model catechetical principles by the way we live our lives.

What makes this book primarily for catechists has to do with how we apply these principles to our lives and to the lives of those we serve, whether they are children, teens, or adults. Being in a truly loving relationship is one of the most satisfying experiences of a lifetime. And no relationship is as important or as potentially satisfying as the relationship we cultivate together with our Lord. As catechists, we have the additional privilege of helping others build a strong foundation for a life of love and service to God.

There is a wise saying, passed down through the ages: "You can't give what you haven't got!" In the pages that follow, I invite you to consider some important principles for a holistic, Christ-centered spirituality—a spirituality supported by a firm foundation in the Catholic faith. In the process, you will learn the importance of being passionate and joyful in your faith. You will be given opportunities to reconnect with your own sacred stories and to discover how those stories are impacted by the greatest story of all. You will be reminded, once again, what a wonderful tool our Catholic faith is for the purpose of building a strong and loving relationship with the Lord.

You will have a chance to reflect upon your prayer life and to sample prayer techniques based upon your specific interests and talents. You will discover ways to decrease personal anxiety while increasing the power of faith in your life. And no book on spirituality is complete without a section on the topic of forgiveness.

In the final chapter, we will spend some time together considering the grace and energy that come from the spiritual practice of renewing our covenant of love with God each day.

Throughout the book I use storytelling to set the topic and the tone for our exploration. My years of preparation for writing this book have taught me that everyone likes a good story and that nothing works as well as a good story to illustrate the power of a spiritual principle. It is my hope and fervent prayer that you will both enjoy and feel the power of God's Holy Spirit in each of the stories. One of my favorite bishops, Bishop Robert Morneau of the Diocese of Green Bay, Wisconsin, is fond of saying: "Every good story is about conversion!" May these stories—all that they contain and all that they inspire—serve as blessings for your life and provide opportunities for growth and conversion while you strive to find your spiritual direction as a catechist!

# CHAPTER ONE

# A Joy Like Never Before

On my way to the office each morning I jump-start my day by stopping at a local fast food restaurant that brews particularly good coffee. Although the restaurant has a drive-through window, I usually park and go inside. This gives me the opportunity to greet a wonderful woman named Jasmine who works the counter on weekday mornings. She has a smile as wide as the sky, which she presents to everyone who approaches her. From my brief conversations with her, I have learned that she is a Christian. I'm amazed at how seamlessly she connects her faith in God with her unmitigated enthusiasm for life. She is one of the most obvious and effective "evangelizers" I have ever met. I've come to admire the way she effortlessly but powerfully witnesses the goodness of God to everyone she meets.

One morning I entered the restaurant and found a line of eight people ahead of me at the counter. There was Jasmine trying to defuse the anger of a man who was upset about the time it was taking to fill his order. She explained that with two of the cooks and a counter attendant out sick, she and the remaining cook were tasked with all responsibilities. This meant that orders would not be filled as promptly or efficiently as usual. No apology or excuse would assuage the angry customer. He became obnoxious and took his rage out verbally on Jasmine. During his tirade, she never flinched or cowered. Perhaps more remarkably, she never attacked or berated him and never returned his anger.

When he received his order, he muttered angrily as he left the building. The next customer was apologetic as she sought to reassure Jasmine. Jasmine looked her right in the eye and said in a voice loud enough for all of us to hear: "It's OK, I'm all right. That man didn't give me my joy; I'm not going to let him take it away." Then she smiled that wonderful smile.

In that moment, Jasmine's unabashed joy, so obviously connected to the love she feels from and for God, made an impression on me—for life. My life has changed. My story became connected in a very special way to the story of God's love for us all. I will never forget Jasmine or her message for me.

For many years a battle has raged inside me. On one side, there is joy, joy that is fueled by the knowledge that God has blessed me with many gifts in my life, from the talents that I possess to the people I've met, the places I've seen to the possessions I've accrued. I have been born into and subsequently married into wonderful families. People love me—a good number of people—and I love them. On the other side of the "battle line" are guilt and shame. I feel guilty and ashamed because I don't always measure up. I don't always make good choices. I feel I have disappointed God and wonder how I could ever deserve God's love and respect.

However, I have come to realize that these periods of guilt and shame are holding me back from becoming my "best self," the person God has created me to be. That is not to imply that I should ignore my transgressions, those times when I fail to do what is best in the eyes of God; however, I must learn to believe that God doesn't want me to dwell on or obsess over those moments. God wants me to learn from them, grow from them, and then return to focus on the unconditional love being offered to me. I am not being asked to earn my way into heaven. God's love and the many benefits of that love are to be understood as gifts, freely given, as part of a divinely loving relationship.

A number of wonderful people, including my parents, my wife, my daughter, various coworkers, my spiritual directors, and my "fast food friend" Jasmine, have continuously reassured me: "Neither death, nor life, nor angels, nor principalities, nor present things, nor future things, nor powers, nor height, nor depth, or any other creature will be able to separate us from the love of God in Jesus Christ our Lord" (Romans 8:38–39).

I encourage you to read the previous paragraph once again. Read it slowly and reflect upon each line for a moment or two. While every line in Scripture is important, some carry more gravitas than others. For me, the two verses (above) are among the most important in the entire Bible. I say this with some authority, based on my personal experience and the experiences of many who come to me for spiritual direction.

## Our Own Harshest Critics

At some point, almost every individual who enters into spiritual direction with me says something that indicates they are locked in a cycle of guilt or shame that keeps them from opening fully to the love that God has for them. In a way, this is a natural phenomenon. As human beings, we are accustomed to having conditions and limits spelled out for any relationship we enter. This is not necessarily a bad thing. For example, all contracts have specific conditions under which the contract will be valid. If those conditions are not met, the contract may be contested. In personal relationships, conditions are generally stated or implied. For example, my friends will continue to be my friends as long as I continue to show an interest in their lives and don't seriously offend them or do something that would cause them grave danger. If one of those conditions is violated, the friendship may be jeopardized.

However, God does not have a "contract" with us. God has a covenant: a promise to love and care for us, no matter what we say or do. Even if we should turn our backs, the Lord will always be with us, inviting us to return to the relationship. When we begin to see God as the one who will never abandon us, who is our biggest fan, the only one who can and does love us without conditions or restrictions, we are set to begin the experience of a lifetime, the experience of feeling pure joy.

This joy transcends all boundaries and limitations. It is not based on material wealth or position, geographic location, cultural heritage, sexual orientation, age, career or any other distinction.

There is a moment in the musical *West Side Story* when Maria, singing the song "I Feel Pretty," beautifully captures the joy of being in love. Her love for Tony is transformative. In that moment she is ecstatic to be in love with such a wonderful young man, *and* she realizes that she is indeed beautiful. She loves and she is loved! Consider for a moment that we too are loved. We are loved by our very wonderful God: the one true God—Father, Son, and Spirit—who has created us to help build the Reign of God right here on earth. Isn't that amazing? Isn't that something to celebrate with great joy?

As catechists we are always challenged, in the best sense of that word, to live and to act out of that joy. Pope Francis advocates for such joy when he says:

The joy of the Gospel is such that it cannot be taken away from us by anyone or anything (cf. Jn 16:22). The evils of our world—and those of the Church—must not be excuses for diminishing our commitment and our fervor....One of the more serious temptations which stifles boldness and zeal is a defeatism which turns us into querulous and disillusioned pessimists, "sourpusses." » *Evangelii Gaudium*

Gospel joy is one of the primary tools in both evangelization and catechesis. What often draws others to us, those who want to know more about us, is the quality of the joy that can only come from living a life in harmony with the Spirit of God. Moreover, that same quality is what keeps people, whether they are our friends or those we are helping to form in our catechetical sessions, coming back. Jasmine is a prime example. She is a living evangelist and catechist. Even on the coldest winter day, I am compelled to get out of my car and go into the restaurant to experience the sacred grace that she exudes. Her joy is a magnet that draws the grace inside me to the grace inside her. She is a gift from the Holy Spirit.

I begin this book with a chapter on joy because I believe it is a prerequisite for every catechist who hopes to be effective in delivering the message of the gospel to those they catechize. Deep and abiding love, especially when seen in the relationship you as a catechist have with the Lord, is an unmistakable sign that you have something wonderful to share with the student. Such love should inspire great joy! Moreover, it is an exquisite invitation to the student to "come and see" what the Lord has for her or him—that is: love beyond all comprehension and a joy beyond all measure.

**Evidence for the Importance of Joy
in Connection with Spirituality**

In his book titled *Chasing Joy*, Fr. Edward Hays presents convincing evidence for the connection between joy and Christian spirituality. He proposes that when the presence of God saturates the totality of one's being, that should bring about "ecstatic joy" and "unflappable Conviction." God's desire to be infused into every cell of our bodies should "skyrocket us into bliss!" (pp. 48–50).

When our daughter, Laura, was in high school, she participated in a two-week mission trip to the Dominican Republic. In many ways, it was a life-changing experience for her. When I asked her to name her most profound "learning" from the trip, she said, almost without hesitation: "I was amazed by how joyful the people were. They didn't have all the fancy stuff that we have in the United States, but they had strong faith-filled families. They looked out for one another and cared for one another. They were very happy, and they welcomed us with open arms."

This is not meant as a criticism of the wonderful things that many of us are blessed to possess here in the United States, nor is it meant to suggest that physical poverty is a precondition for holiness or joy. However, it does demonstrate that true joy is not connected to material wealth but to values such as love and faith. We could not have taught our daughter this lesson as effectively as did the mission trip.

In *Chasing Joy*, Hays is careful to remind us that living a life of joy does not mean we will always feel happy or that our life will be free of tribulations and discomfort. It doesn't mean living in a state of perpetual bliss. What it does mean is simply that living in the embrace of God, with certainty that our best friend, the Lord, is always with us, can generally have such a calming and reassuring effect that we will sustain a measure of hope and joyfulness no matter the circumstances we face.

Moreover, Catholicism teaches that all of God's creation—the sun, the moon, the stars, our world and all who inhabit it—is sacred. We are surrounded by beauty. In his *Spiritual Exercises*, Saint Ignatius reminds us: "All the things in this world are gifts from God, presented to us so that we can know God more easily and make a return of love more readily."

In his book *Between Heaven and Mirth: Why Joy, Humor and Laughter Are at the Heart of the Spiritual Life*, Fr. James Martin, SJ, reveals the fruits of his fascinating research concerning joy and spirituality:

> When I started to study joy, I was overwhelmed. It is an immense field of scholarly research. The theme of joy runs throughout almost all the major religions and spiritual traditions. In the Old Testament, the people of Israel express their joy to God for having delivered them from slavery. In the Gospels, Jesus often uses that very word as a way of expressing a goal of discipleship. Later, St. Paul encourages the early Christians to "rejoice always." Joy is one of the traditional "fruits of the Holy Spirit," that is, gifts from God given to build us up. Even if many religions don't seem particularly joyful, the religious literature on the topic is vast.  » *Between Heaven and Mirth*, p. 24

A good friend introduced me to a profound statement by Presbyterian minister Frederick Buechner: "The place God calls you to is the place where your deep gladness and the world's deep hunger meet." I have seen this statement verified, time and again, in the lives of young (and not so young) adults with whom I have worked. In fact, I can honestly say that I have seen the fruits of this statement in my own life.

In the movie *Chariots of Fire*, the protagonist, a remarkable Scottish runner and Olympic medalist named Eric Liddell, is asked why he loves to run. His reply is both spiritual and profoundly joyful: "When I run, I feel His pleasure." It's a beautiful testimony to the loving relationship that Liddell has with God and to his tremendous joy in using his talent to give glory to the Lord.

Be cheered by the knowledge that, when problems such as student disciplinary issues, time constraints, or difficulty in finding resources threaten to rob you of the joy of being a catechist, Jesus (the Master Catechist) is with you, to give you courage, guidance, and joy.

I hope you are able to feel the pleasure that God receives from your ministry. Moreover, I pray that you feel tremendous joy—the joy that comes from knowing that you are using gifts that have been bestowed uniquely upon you in order to give honor and glory to God. Always remember that you are working to ensure that the gospel message will be cherished and lived for generations to come in those whom you catechize. And when challenging circumstances arise in your ministry or your life, remember the one who has given you your joy—to cherish and to share!

**FOR REFLECTION AND DISCUSSION**

• Choose one or two of these quotes about joy that you find particularly appealing. What is it about the quote that speaks to you?

*"We must attract them by joy in order to lead them to its source, the Heart of Christ."* » ST. KATHARINE DREXEL

*"A cheerful heart is good medicine, but a downcast spirit dries up the bones."* » PROVERBS 17:22

*"Rejoice always!"* » PHILIPPIANS 4:4

- Recall a time when you felt great joy connected with some aspect of your spiritual life. It might have been during a catechetical session, a time of prayer, a sacramental celebration, etc. Pause to remember as many details about the experience as possible. What do you think contributed to the joy? What are you feeling and thinking as you recall the occasion? If possible, share this story with someone close to you—a family member, friend, fellow catechist, etc.

- Have you ever met someone who radiates the joy of the Lord? What do you feel when you are in the presence of that person? If you desired to become more like that person, what do you think you would need to do?

## PRAYING WITH SCRIPTURE

LUKE 15:1–10 • JOHN 16:22 • ROMANS 8:38–39 • ROMANS 14:16–17

## PRAYING WITH MUSIC *(available on YouTube)*

**"Joyful, Joyful, We Adore Thee"** | *Henry van Dyke, Ludwig van Beethoven*
(WWW.YOUTUBE.COM/WATCH?V=EMY3IVDNZWE)

**"Good to Be Alive"** | *Jason Gray*
(WWW.YOUTUBE.COM/WATCH?V=4OMFQJEAAVC)

**"Alive"** | *Natalie Grant*
(WWW.YOUTUBE.COM/WATCH?V=W1GZOUNUN20)

**"How Can I Keep from Singing?"** | *Robert Lowry*
(WWW.YOUTUBE.COM/WATCH?V=CNSCKKVEQNU)

# CHAPTER TWO

# Catholicism: The Faith I Love to Practice

A primary reason for my love of Catholicism is the way we are taught to view the world. Our faith is based on the principle that the world and all that is in it are gifts from God. Indeed, the world holds the seeds of the Kingdom/Reign of God. As Catholics we are called, by virtue of our baptism, to become what Pope Francis and others have called "missionary disciples." This means we are to use the many gifts that we find in the world, as well as the gifts and talents that we possess within us, to help construct this Reign of God right here, right now.

The Reign of God is here with us but not yet complete. Our charge is to keep working, striving to bring justice and peace to all nations and all peoples. In Scripture, God has given us the model for our missionary work in the message and the person of Jesus Christ. Jesus taught us about love of God, neighbor, and self, gave us the Beatitudes, and reinforced the importance of the Ten Commandments handed down to us through Moses.

The Blessed Trinity—Father, Son, and Holy Spirit—has guided the church through the ages, outlining additional details for building the Reign of God and using the wisdom and understanding of many holy people, some of whom we now know as saints, to guide us along the way. In his book *What Makes Us Catholic: Eight Gifts for Life*, Thomas Groome writes: "The Trinity means that God is always at work in the world—creating, liberating and sanctifying—and inviting our responsible participation in God's dream for us all. That's what life is all about!" (p. 90).

## Swimming in a Sea of Grace

The world's innate goodness is described beautifully by Saint Ignatius Loyola: "All the things in this world are gifts of God, created for us, to be the means by which we can come to know him better, love him more surely and serve him more faithfully…As a result, we ought to appreciate and use these gifts…."

Such a recognition of the goodness in God's creation seems to contradict some teaching in Scripture, especially in the writings of Saints Paul and James, where, on occasion, we find them referring to the world as a place that is not "of God." For example:

- Has not God made the wisdom of the world foolish?
  » 1 CORINTHIANS 1:20
- We have not received the spirit of the world but the Spirit that is from God, so that we may understand the things freely given us by God. » 1 CORINTHIANS 2:12

And in the Epistle of James, we read:

- Therefore, whoever wants to be a lover of the world makes himself an enemy of God. » JAMES 4:4

How does one reconcile this discrepancy? It seems to me that when Saints Paul and James refer to the world with such a negative tone, they are not talking about the world that God created (which includes human beings, created in God's image and likeness). Rather they are referring to the notion of a world without God. This can be likened to our contemporary use of the term "worldly" as conveying someone or something rooted in a secular context that ignores the spiritual realm.

Evidence for the creation of worldly "idols" is prevalent, even today. "The dominant attitude of society," says Groome, "is that our worth depends on what we do, possess, or achieve. Christian faith, by contrast, holds that the worthwhileness of life…does not depend on our efforts alone. Rather, life in the world is worthwhile because of God's providence, presence, and partnership with us" (Groome, p. 83). The great gifts of God that we find all around us in the world are part of the divine master plan to reach out to us and invite us to fall ever more deeply in love with God.

So it is that we can look at a bee pollinating a plant, a spider weaving an intricate web, and a robin building a nest as examples of the grandeur of God. We can also be touched by the intimacy of a mother holding her child to her breast, a father embracing his son upon his return from a long and arduous separation, a priest at Mass raising the consecrated bread and wine—the Body and Blood of Christ—as examples of the deep love that we are called to recognize and appreciate as part of what it means to be fully alive. We are swimming in a sea of grace, overwhelmed by the great goodness of God. We are gifted beyond measure, and we are called to be gift to one another.

## We Are Blessed to Be Co-Creators

The wonderful world into which each of us is born carries with it certain responsibilities. We are all given gifts and talents in order to bring about the Reign of God here on earth. Participating in this exciting and fulfilling process qualifies us, cooperating with the grace of God, as co-creators.

This has profound and wonderful implications for catechists. We can begin by identifying the particular gifts we bring to our catechetical ministry. This might include gifts such as a passion for the faith, a keen intellect, the ability to recognize the unique nature of each student, a creative approach to lesson planning, empathy for all whom we teach, joyful and encouraging personalities, a talent for organizing and explaining the content of the lessons, a knack for classroom management, or the ability to challenge students toward excellence.

These are just a few of the many possible gifts that a catechist may bring to her or his role. But none of us possesses all of them. Each of us has a different mixture of gifts and each gift is a resource to be used when we accept our role as co-creators of God's Reign.

We are called to put our faith to work by engaging wholeheartedly in the process of living each day with integrity, purpose, and love. In doing so, we weave our faith into the fabric of our being. It becomes a guidepost for how we will engage the people and circumstances in which we find ourselves each day. This premise then leads us to another profound concept: what Fr. James Bacik has labeled "situational spirituality."

### A Faith for All Seasons

Fr. Bacik bases the concept of situational spirituality on the work of Jesuit theologian Karl Rahner. Rahner, a twentieth-century German priest, was one of the architects of the documents of the Second Vatican Council.

According to Bacik, Rahner has three main assumptions that serve as the foundation for his theology. These are very important for an understanding of situational spirituality. They are as follows:

1. We (human beings) are oriented toward mystery...we are
   wired for God. We are restlessly searching for the meaning
   of life. St. Augustine framed it in these words: "Our souls are
   restless, Lord, until they rest in you." Another way to express
   this is to say that we long for an intimate relationship with
   the infinite (God).
2. We are interdependent...social creatures. We are called to
   love others and to allow ourselves to be loved by others...and
   especially by God.
3. Our outlook regarding creation is basically good. One could
   say: The grace of God interpenetrates us because we are each
   "Temples of the Holy Spirit."

To develop situational spirituality, one begins by asking questions
such as the following: What am I dealing with? Where is God in
this process? What would God want me to learn from this situation? By doing so, we are letting our lives write the agenda for
our spiritual journeys. At this point, anything and everything that
we experience has the potential to speak to us about God. Author
Paula D'Arcy expresses this principle in one beautiful sentence:
"God comes to us disguised as our lives."

God can and does speak to us in myriad ways at countless times
during the course of any given day. We begin to realize and understand this process once we have trained ourselves, with the help
of God's grace, to have "eyes to see and ears to hear." This is one of
the most important spiritual principles we can teach our children,
youth, and adults.

When we embrace the idea that God is always with us, loving us
unconditionally, we can celebrate that we are never alone. Our very

best friend is always with us. This is a key principle in developing a personal relationship with the Lord.

Rafaela was a wonderful woman of faith who served as a catechetical leader at a parish I visited while working for a diocesan catechetical office many years ago. I was so impressed with her faith, her character, and her love for God (as well as her love for the children in her program) that I wondered if perhaps she might be part human and part angel. This would befit her name—a female version of the name for the angel Raphael. One day during a conversation about her faith, she told me: "I do a lot of driving. Living out here in the country, I am not particularly close to anything, except the church, which you can see from my window. Sometimes, when I am cruising down the highway by myself, I will gently put my hand over on the passenger seat next to me. I imagine Jesus sitting there, and we talk. We talk about all sorts of things, whatever happens to be on my mind on that particular day."

For Rafaela, Jesus was with her everywhere, all the time. He made his presence known in her life via the people with whom she communicated and the situations she encountered each day. Jesus was her very best friend. And the love that they shared gave her profound joy and courage. Her faith was made more relevant and vibrant as she practiced situational spirituality. Moreover, her attitude was contagious. Catechists loved teaching in her program because she was such a witness to them and to the students. She impacted many a life for Christ by her very nature.

### The Seven Sacraments: Mountaintop Experiences

One of the most important developments in our Catholic understanding of the world has been the identification of our seven sacraments. These seven specific gifts to us are part of a larger theological construct sometimes referred to as the principle of sacramentality. In *What Makes Us Catholic*, Groome has written eloquently on this subject. In his construct, the principle of sacramentality fits perfectly with the concept of situational spirituality. The principle means:

> God is present to humankind and we respond to God's grace through the ordinary and everyday of life in the world...
>
> Understood within the sacramentality of life in the world, the seven sacraments are sacred symbols that mediate God's grace in Jesus with heightened effect...Catholic Christians should never think of the seven sacraments as apart from life. All must be appreciated as apex moments that heighten and celebrate the sacramentality of life in the world. » *What Makes Us Catholic*, pp. 84–85

The elements of this world, created by God, have a significant part in the celebration of the various sacraments. For example, wheat, grapes, water, oil, and fire each have an important role to play in our worship experience. Moreover, the actions of the senses: smelling, touching, tasting, hearing, and seeing are all engaged. God is giving us the profound signal that the things of his world are to be used to deepen our relationship with God and with one another. Noted theologian Rosemary Haughton says it this way: "Sacraments are extraordinary experiences of the ordinary" (Groome, p. 85).

The seven sacraments are distinctive ways God comes to meet us, dwelling among us in the world. And the sacrament that all other sacraments point us toward is the Eucharist.

The gift of the Eucharist—which can properly be called both the sacrifice of the Mass and the celebration of Christ's life, death, and resurrection (the paschal mystery)—is the source and summit of our faith. The Eucharist is the sacrament around which everything else revolves. It is the activity that gives meaning to all that we are called to say, do, and be as Catholic Christians. It is no accident that Christ chose a meal at which to institute this great gift—the gift of his very self. After all, meals are events around which we celebrate so many of the most important activities of our lives: from the very basic necessity of nourishing our bodies with the strength that food provides, to the desire for celebrating significant events like birthdays, anniversaries, and the many occasions that call for a joyous gathering of people. Jesus recognized that mealtime is, quite simply, the time to be fed. Thus, he established the Eucharist as the primary source of our spiritual nourishment.

As catechists, we are compelled to devote ourselves to participation in the Eucharist—a source of spiritual nourishment like no other. Our participation in the Eucharist serves to strengthen our love for the Lord and our resolve to go forth and give witness, throughout the world, to God's goodness and mercy. The Catholic Church, aided by two thousand years of lived experience and guided by the Holy Spirit, has placed this beautiful and profound sacrament at the center of the practice of our faith.

## A Rich Tapestry: Enduring and Endearing

It stands to reason that Catholicism, a way of believing that puts great emphasis on the beauty and wonder of God's creation, would therefore encourage and support the care and stewardship of this wonderful world—a place we are visiting on the way to our eternal home. You will notice, I refer to it as God's world. There is a tendency, popular among many people in the twenty-first century, to think of this as *our* world, as in "the world that we own." Such thinking is both arrogant and dangerous. We are called to be stewards of God's creation, protecting humanity and all of the natural resources of this world from unjust treatment and exploitation. The Catholic Church has taken an active role in attempting to protect creation. In the past two centuries alone, papal encyclicals such as *Rerum Novarum* (Of New Things, Pope Leo XIII, 1891), *Sollicitudo Rei Socialis* (The Social Concern of the Church, Saint Pope John Paul II, 1987), *Caritas in Veritate* (Charity in Truth, Pope Benedict XVI, 2009), and *Laudato Si'* (On Care for Our Common Home, Pope Francis, 2015) have emphasized this stewardship. Here in the United States, the documents *Economic Justice for All*, *The Challenge of Peace*, and *Our Hearts Were Burning within Us* by the American bishops echo this call to stewardship. Moreover, "The Catholic Climate Covenant" has garnered a huge following of Catholics and members of other faith groups who are concerned about the future of our planet (www.catholicclimatecovenant.org).

Internationally known Catholic activists such as St. Vincent de Paul, St. Teresa of Calcutta, and Dorothy Day have been at the forefront in caring for the poor and disenfranchised. Religious orders, including congregations of priests, brothers, and women religious have for centuries practiced the spiritual and corporal works of mercy on a daily basis as a way to care for all of God's creation. And countless numbers of the faithful have volunteered their time, talent, and treasure to support a myriad of causes that assist those in need.

Catholicism has given us a tried and true road map for living a life of sacred purpose. As catechists, we have a multitude of wonderful people, organizations, and documents from which to gather knowledge about and inspiration from this faith we love to practice. The more we know about the teachings of the church, and the more we strive to integrate those teachings into our lives, the more committed we will be to our catechetical mission—that is, to help others grow to love the faith and to practice it with passion and joy!

## FOR REFLECTION AND DISCUSSION

- Who mentored you in the development of your faith? Perhaps it was a parent, a grandparent, an aunt, or an uncle. Maybe it was a priest or a teacher or a close friend. What was it about that person that made them such an important contributor to your spiritual development? Have you ever thanked that individual for the significant role they have played in your life?

- As a catechist, what aspects of Catholicism do you particularly enjoy teaching and/or talking about with your students? Why do these topics give you so much energy and joy?

- Name some ways you would like to grow in your knowledge of Catholicism: both for your own benefit and for the benefit of those you teach. How will you pursue such growth?

## PRAYING WITH SCRIPTURE

MARK 14:22–25 • JOHN 6:31–35 • JOHN 6:47–51 • ACTS 2:42

## PRAYING WITH MUSIC *(available on YouTube)*

**"Gather Us In"** | *Marty Haugen*
(WWW.YOUTUBE.COM/WATCH?V=HULORIYEET4&LIST=RDHULORIYEET4)

**"Remembrance"** | *Matt Maher*
(WWW.YOUTUBE.COM/WATCH?V=CFDE8SPRZWS)

**"How Beautiful"** | *Twila Paris*
(WWW.YOUTUBE.COM/WATCH?V=Y8ZONBMFAT8)

**"In the Breaking of the Bread"** | *Bob Hurd, Michael Downey*
(WWW.YOUTUBE.COM/WATCH?V=XVC2E7IDF2G)

CHAPTER THREE

# Life Is a Prayer

What do you mean when you say that you love God? Love is a complicated word. It is used in many different ways. I have been known to say: "I love that candy bar!" and "I love that car!" However, that kind of "love" is a far cry from the loving relationship that we are invited to cultivate with God. Our love for God should be more like "falling in love"—not in a sexual context, but in a deeply spiritual context that can include moments of ecstasy as we appreciate how much we are loved and cared for and how much we desire to give ourselves over to the will of God. Prayer, in one form or another, is the primary way we communicate with God and God with us.

Prayer involves both talking and listening. Intimacy in a friendship increases as we share our thoughts and feelings openly and honestly, with sincerity and trust, and as we give and receive love and support. Since God is *always* calling us to move deeper into this wonderful loving relationship, it makes sense that God provides us with ample opportunities to do so. And, just as with any meaningful relationship, a spiritual relationship doesn't happen overnight. It takes great care and dedication.

So how does one cultivate this very special loving relationship with God? The process begins with awareness. St. Ignatius suggested that we must train ourselves to find God in all things: in people, in works of art and nature, as well as in those places (like a church) where we customarily think of God.

Many years ago, I attended a marvelous workshop where the instructor hung a series of thirty magazine pictures on the walls of the classroom. He asked each of us to find one picture that captured some characteristic of God. There were photographs of people as well as beautiful landscapes and inanimate objects. One woman chose a picture of an interaction between an adult (quite possibly a parent) and a child. There was obviously great love and affection being shared. She explained why she chose the picture: "I see love here. God is love."

I have conducted this exercise many times over the years with various age groups, using slides. The exercise opens the door to further conversation about the grandeur of God and the many ways we can be reminded of God, if we have "eyes to see." It is intriguing to observe how two people can pick the very same picture yet see two completely different metaphors for God. Because each person brings her or his own story (own set of experiences) to the picture, each has a unique interpretation.

Hand in hand with the process of becoming aware of God's presence throughout creation is the attitude of gratitude. Meister Eckhart, a thirteenth-century Dominican monk, said: "If the only prayer you ever say in your entire life is thank you, it will be enough." St. Paul also reinforces the importance of gratitude: "Pray without ceasing. In all circumstances give thanks, for this is the will of God for you in Christ Jesus" (1 Thessalonians 5:17–18).

**Prayers Are Many and Splendid Things**

There are numerous ways to pray, and each one provides the opportunity for great creativity. I often begin lessons on prayer with the question: "How would you define the term 'prayer'?" Generally, I receive responses like: "Prayer is talking to God." "Prayer is reading Scripture." "The Mass is a prayer." Certainly, these are forms of prayer, or ways to describe prayer. However, prayer entails so many different forms and expressions that it is difficult to describe them all. A number of years ago, theologian Charles J. Keating wrote a book titled: *Who We Are Is How We Pray*. If we assume this to be true, the numbers of ways to pray are unique and almost limitless.

Prayer can be rote or spontaneous. Prayer can be spoken, read, sung, written (the use of a journal), or silent (as in meditation or contemplation). Moreover, prayer can be offered for a variety of reasons: giving thanks, praising, petitioning, offering, expressing love, dedicating, blessing, etc. And our ability to pray can be enhanced by the attitude/disposition that we bring to prayer. When we see life as a gift, creation as good, people as sacred, work as holy, and suffering as something that can lead to growth, we open ourselves to the possibility of a more profound experience of prayer.

It is important to respect the various ways people pray. Some have moments of deep communion with God by saying the Rosary. Other people find their greatest comfort in praying spontaneously to God, in their own words, letting God know exactly what is on their minds and in their hearts. Respect and reverence for the prayer style of each individual is something we are all called to practice.

In his book *Prayer: Our Deepest Longing*, Ronald Rohlheiser writes:

> If you begin to feel anxious or to worry that you are not
> "doing it right," remember the words of a holy peasant who,
> when asked to share his secret to deep prayer said simply,

"I just look at God, and I let God look at me." Anyone who has ever been in love will know the power of those words. It is enough to be relaxed and quiet in the presence of God, ready to receive and return God's loving glance. » p. 69

Our Catholic faith teaches us that our forms of prayer should include both communal prayer and individual prayer. It is not an "either/or" proposition. Of course, some of our most beautiful prayers, such as the Our Father and the Hail Mary, can be said in both a communal and an individual setting. As catechists, make sure your students learn these and other beautiful prayers of the church. This is a terrific way to help them focus on a multitude of wonderful images and important faith concepts that have been handed down to us over many centuries.

Some forms of prayer, like the need to get comfortable and simply talk with God about what is on one's mind, are best realized by finding and identifying that favorite "prayer spot," the place where one goes in order to be alone with God. I believe that every person in every household should have a particular spot for enjoying quiet time with the Lord. Moreover, it does not need to be within the house. It may be on the deck, in the backyard, or at a park down the street. I vividly remember the small secluded park I visited during my college years, when I was in need of a lovely, quiet place in which to have a heart-to-heart conversation with the Lord. Some of the most significant decisions of my young adult life were made in that beautiful spot.

Of course, a chapter on prayer would not be complete without mentioning the Mass. As members of the body of Christ, when we come together as a community to worship the Lord, we unite our spirits with one another, and with God, in the most profound form of prayer.

It is very important to teach the details regarding what we do at Mass and why it is so important. Moreover, we must take great care to make sure that parents as well as their children hear this message; for it is the parents who have the significant responsibility of seeing that both they and their children attend Mass.

However, as catechists we are commissioned to do more than simply impart the "what and how" of the Mass. We lead most effectively by example. Full participation in the celebration of the Eucharist empowers us, by the grace of God, to enrich our spiritual life. In the process, our lives are renewed and we become living witnesses to the significance of the Eucharist as the ultimate form of prayer.

### Additional Prayers that Can Shape the Life of a Catechist

*Praying with Scripture*—Scripture serves as the foundation for the beliefs and practices of our faith. As catechists, all that we teach has roots in the word of the Lord. We do well to remember that the Bible provides a great source of knowledge and inspiration for our own faith formation and the formation of those we catechize. Here are two specific practices that feature the Bible as a focal point for prayer: *lectio divina* and gospel contemplation.

The practice of *lectio divina* ("divine reading") was first described and practiced in the twelfth century. It is a way of reading the Scriptures whereby we gradually let go of our own prayer agenda and "open our hearts and minds to what God wants to say to us" ("What Is Lectio Divina": http://ocarm.org/en/content/lectio/what-lectio-divina).

*Lectio divina* (sometimes abbreviated to "*lectio*") can be practiced with various nuances. However, the most common form involves four movements:

1. *Lectio* (reading)—Select a passage from Scripture and read it aloud, slowly and reflectively. This might be a passage

from the liturgy of the day, the upcoming Sunday liturgy, or perhaps a random passage. (A passage of approximately 8–15 verses is ideal.)

2. *Meditatio* (reflection)—After reading the passage, select a word, phrase, or sentence that speaks to you personally. Spend several minutes meditating on it in order to take from it what you feel God is saying.

3. *Oratio* (response)—Simply speak to God about whatever is on your mind or in your heart at this point. (Your response should be inspired by your reflection on the Scripture.)

4. *Contemplatio* (rest)—Let go of every thought that has been part of the process to this point and simply rest in God's loving embrace. Attempt to clear your mind so that you can "listen" at the deepest level of your being. Trust that the still small voice that enlightens your mind/heart at this point will work with your open and trusting spirit to guide whatever action, conversion, or transformation is being presented for your consideration.

[**NOTE:** *Often, when you use this process in a group setting, you can invite (but never force) each member of the group to respond aloud at various stages of the process, regarding the part of the reading that is prompting that person to prayer and deeper reflection.*]

When choosing to use Scripture for any prayer activity, remember this important guiding principle: "The word of God is alive and active and will transform each of us if we open ourselves to receive what God wants to give us" ("What Is Lectio Divina?").

*Gospel contemplation* is a form of prayer made popular by St. Ignatius "in which one uses his or her senses in an imaginative way to reflect upon a Gospel passage. Use the senses, seeing, hearing, tasting, touching, and smelling to make the Gospel scene real and alive" (http://www.ignatianspirituality.com/ignatian-prayer/the-what-how-why-of-prayer/praying-with-scripture).

[**NOTE:** *This is not to be confused with the term "contemplative prayer," a form of prayer that espouses "emptying the mind" and is also called "centering prayer." Fr. Thomas Keating is a proponent of that prayer style.*]

Gospel contemplation has several stages/movements.

1.  Select a passage from one of the gospels in which Jesus is interacting with others.

2.  Remember, prayer forms that use Scripture, such as *lectio divina* and gospel contemplation are about listening for God's word(s) to you. Let God be the "actor" and allow yourself to be the recipient.

3.  Read the gospel passage twice (aloud, if possible) so that you become very familiar with it.

4.  Close your eyes and reconstruct the scene with as much detail as possible. Feel free to use your imagination to fill in details not given in the story. Moreover, consider imagining you are a character in the story. Begin by merely observing, but become an active member of the story if you feel called to do so. In the process, ask yourself some questions about what you are witnessing, such as: What are people saying? What feelings are they expressing? Is Jesus touching anyone? What is the result of Jesus' touch? What am I thinking and/or feeling as a result of my participation in the story?

5.  If you feel you don't really have an active imagination, do not worry. You can still engage the story at your own level. Just try to be open to wherever God's prompting takes you in the

process. Vividness is not a criterion for this type of prayer.

6. Finish your prayer with a short conversation directly with Jesus, saying whatever comes from your heart. (Adapted from *Finding God in All Things: A Marquette Prayer Book*, noted in Praying with Scripture, on ignatianspirituality.com)

*Music as an "Instrument" for Prayer*—There is an ancient maxim often attributed to St. Augustine, which states: "He who sings prays twice." When we sing, play, or listen to music, we enter into prayer at a profound level. The emotive nature of music calls forth feelings and thoughts. It takes us to places in the heart where we might not otherwise go. It evokes emotions that can deepen the experience of prayer.

Music is a language unto itself. The combination of various notes, the rise and fall of the volume, the appealing nature of the beat, the pace of the delivery of the message—all of these things, added to the power of the lyrics, can contribute to a profoundly spiritual experience.

Catechists can use music to reinforce lessons of faith in their classrooms. Usually they begin by finding a song that speaks to them about the theme of the lesson; then they create discussion questions that will help the students mine the song for meaning. Not only is this activity beneficial for teaching the students, but it reinforces faith formation for the catechist as well.

*The Examen*—One of the prayer exercises of St. Ignatius is called the Daily Examen, Examination of Consciousness, or simply the Examen. This is something slightly different than the examination of conscience used before celebrating the sacrament of reconciliation. In the Daily Examen, the participant mentally reviews the events of the day to see where the goodness of God was particularly present or where the participant failed to appreciate and act upon

God's wisdom and grace. It is a simple and beautiful way to call to mind that God is in the midst of our day, even though we might not have realized it at the time.

Here is a quick and easy way to practice this meaningful prayer:

1. In the evening, find a quiet place to meditate by looking back on the events of the day in the company of the Holy Spirit. If parts of the day are confusing or if you cannot remember some aspects, ask God to bring clarity and understanding.

2. Review the day with a grateful heart. Remember, prayer is best begun with an attitude of gratitude. As you walk through the day, note the times of joy and delight. Focus on the day's gifts. Consider the work you accomplished and the people with whom you interacted. What did you receive from them? What did you give to them? Think about the details of the day, such as what you ate, what you saw, etc., remembering that God is in the details.

3. Pay attention to your emotions. One of the many great insights of St. Ignatius was his realization that we can often detect the presence of the Holy Spirit in the movements of our emotions. Take time to reflect on the various emotions you experienced during the day. How might God have been speaking to you through those emotions?

4. Choose a specific feature of the day and pray it. Ask the Holy Spirit to guide you to a particular thought, feeling, or encounter from the day. It may be something striking or something that seemed insignificant at the time. Follow where the Spirit leads, and take some time to pray about it. Allow the prayer to arise spontaneously from your heart, whether it is a prayer of intercession, praise, repentance, gratitude, surrender, or petition.

5. Look toward tomorrow. Ask God to give you wisdom and strength for the challenges the next day may present. Pay attention to the feelings that surface as you think about it. Are you excited, delighted, doubtful, anxious, or reluctant? Allow yourself to form these feelings into prayer(s). Seek God's guidance, pray for hope, courage or whatever you feel is needed for the situations you may face. St. Ignatius encouraged people to talk to God as a friend. (Does that sound familiar?) Sometime during the process, take a few moments to ask the Lord for forgiveness for your sins. And don't forget to do all of this in a spirit of gratitude. If time allows, end your Examen with the Our Father.

*[adapted from "How Can I Pray?" Daily Examen. Loyola Press: ignatianspirituality.com, 2017]*

St. Pope John XXIII prayed the Examen twice a day—at midday and at bedtime. He was afraid that if he waited until retiring to perform his first Examen of the day he would forget too much of what happened that morning. (I can relate to that!) He wanted to constantly remind himself that God was clearly in the middle of everything that he was experiencing.

## Prayer Is a Miracle

God has provided us with an almost infinite number of ways to "go deeper" in expressing and receiving the love and affection that is part of a healthy and ever more beautiful relationship. However, on occasion we will find it difficult to pray. For any number of reasons, from fatigue to depression, from anger to frustration, from trepidation to temptation, we will simply be unable to muster the energy, the desire, or perhaps the faith to pray.

Not long ago, a catechist came to me with a story about her inability to pray. Her husband had been seriously ill for a number of weeks and she found herself drained, both physically and emotionally. Her situation was compounded by feeling guilty because she was not praying, and even guiltier because she didn't even have the desire to pray.

Ignatius had a suggestion for such circumstances—asking for "the desire to pray." At first glance, this suggestion may sound naïve or simple-minded; however, it has great merit. When I pray for the desire to pray, I feel that God is pleased with my openness and will help me to overcome the barrier to prayer. This resonates with a beautiful line from a poem (dedicated to God) by twentieth-century monk and mystic Thomas Merton, who wrote: "I believe that the desire to please you does in fact please you."

As a catechist for many years, I have had the opportunity to teach religion in both PSR (parish school of religion) and Catholic school settings. When I was a young catechist, it took me a while to learn how to handle the behavioral challenges posed by certain students. I would pray desperately to God for help, but I was too frantic and panicked to really listen for the answers to my prayers. When I began to relax a bit, stop criticizing myself, and seek the wise counsel of veteran teachers/catechists, I found a great deal of helpful advice and resources. In retrospect, I am sure God was trying to show me a way to proceed, but I wasn't listening carefully to what is sometimes "a still small voice."

Prayer is a miracle! It is an amazing activity of the spirit, a moment in time when the spirit in each one of us meets and touches the Spirit of God. Like the beautiful Michelangelo painting on the ceiling of the Sistine Chapel in which God and humankind reach out to touch one another, prayer is beautiful; it is priceless, a miracle in and of itself, made possible by the grace of God!

## FOR REFLECTION AND DISCUSSION

- How do you like to pray? (Name as many ways that you pray as you can name.)

- Do you have a particular place where you like to pray? What makes that place an especially good "prayer place" for you?

- When have you struggled to be able to pray? What were the circumstances? What (if anything) helped you get back "into prayer"?

- When you talk with your students about prayer, what do you try to emphasize?

- Prayer also involves listening. In a society that rewards activity and busyness, how do we teach the value of being quiet and simply listening for the voice of God?

## PRAYING WITH SCRIPTURE

1 KINGS 20:11–13  •  PSALM 102:13–23  •  MATTHEW 6:9–13

1 THESSALONIANS 5:17–18

## PRAYING WITH MUSIC *(available on YouTube)*

**"Center of My Life"**  |  *Paul Inwood and The Grail (GIA)*
(WWW.YOUTUBE.COM/WATCH?V=B5ZO548RT8O)

**"Word of God Speak"**  |  *Mercy Me*
(WWW.YOUTUBE.COM/WATCH?V=DPOZEDO9OB0)

**"Thy Word"**  |  *Amy Grant*
(WWW.YOUTUBE.COM/WATCH?V=9OTVUGAITSE)

**"Holy Spirit"**  |  *Francesca Battistelli*
(WWW.YOUTUBE.COM/WATCH?V=UVBBC7-PSHO)

# CHAPTER FOUR

# Free Will and God's Will

When I was young I loved to sing. I had several favorite radio stations that played rock and roll. I knew most of the songs by heart, and I sang them loud and long all over the house. I also sang along with the radio when listening with my friends. In eighth grade, I was told that I had a nice voice. At that point I decided to sing in public.

So when I was a freshman in high school, I auditioned for the school musical. I was an Irish tenor, but I was also a "late bloomer." I was very small for my age, and my voice had not yet changed. I was a skinny kid with self-esteem issues and a high soprano-like voice that got higher when I was nervous. After listening to my audition, the music director, a young man with a very acerbic wit, made a joke about my appearance and my voice. He said I had "activated the maternal instinct in all of the female students at the audition." I was crushed! Not only was I told that there was no role for me in the play, but I soon realized that my new-found notoriety as the "pipsqueak with the voice of a girl" did not endear me to any of the "cool kids" in my class. Moreover, that infamous title was going to make it much more difficult to get a date with any of the young ladies in the room.

Over the years I managed to overcome my embarrassment and sing in a number of choirs. However, I was still reluctant to sing a solo. I thought I had a decent voice and felt I was being called to offer it back to God as the gift I knew it was. With that in mind, I mustered the courage to ask our parish music director for an audition to serve as a cantor/song leader in our parish. She gently walked me through the audition and then trained me as a cantor. I have been serving in that capacity for a number of years now and deriving great joy from offering the gift of my voice for the purpose of worshiping God. I have come full circle from the day when I was roundly humiliated to the day when I could give glory to God with my voice. No doubt, God was deeply hurt when I was hurt but promised that I would have other opportunities to use my gift. I like to imagine a smile on the face of Christ when, after preparation and prayer, I offer this gift of music to him.

I use this story to illustrate one of the most important spiritual principles you bring to your ministry as a catechist. God created each of us with free will. However, the gift of free will can sometimes be very difficult to bear when it is used to deprive us of something we think we deserve. The clever but cutting music director chose to make a demeaning remark about my voice. I chose to allow his words to offend me. For many years thereafter I chose not to attempt to sing a solo. Eventually, I overcame my anxiety sufficiently in order to audition for the liturgical role of cantor. Our parish director of music chose to accept and to train me. I believe that during each one of these choices God was present, empathizing with me and offering comfort and support—rejoicing when I rejoiced and sharing my pain when I was suffering, as any "best friend" would do.

The gift of free will is what differentiates us, as human beings, from puppets on a string. Even though free will can be used to make poor (and at times even evil) decisions, God has given this gift, because without it we would not have the privilege of making our own decisions. A truly loving relationship is one in which each individual honors and respects the rights and responsibilities of the other person. It entails the ability to choose for oneself and to experience the good and/or the bad consequences of one's choices.

The gift of free will empowers us to make choices about the career we will pursue, if and who we will marry, where we will live, how we will choose to serve others, and hundreds of other choices we make every day. Linked with the gifts of reason and intelligence, it allows us to enter into that wonderful process of being co-creators with God. We become partners with God in the process of building God's reign here on earth.

God chose to gift us with free will, thereby choosing not to control our thoughts or actions. I believe God was also saying, in essence, the only way we are going to be able to learn and to grow as human beings is if we are allowed to make our own choices and to then reflect upon them, learn from them, and grow with them.

### Actions Have Consequences

Our daughter, Laura, is now in her mid-thirties. A few years ago, I asked her to name a specific lesson about life that she learned from her mother and me. Without hesitating, she said: "Actions have consequences." That's another important "learning," directly related to the concept of free will.

Let's revisit my story for a moment. It would be easy to dismiss its outcome by simply saying I did not get the part in the musical because God had other plans for me. Indeed, if we accept the idea that God knows all things, God knew that I was not going to get the part and that I was going to be totally humiliated in the process. However, the fact that God possessed such knowledge does not necessarily mean that God wanted those things to happen to me. God was not the music teacher who got a huge laugh from the joke he chose to make at my expense.

If we are to appreciate the depth of the love that God has for us, we must understand the significance of free will and how the decisions that we, and others, make can and often do have a major impact on us. While God is present in all aspects of our lives, God is not the causal agent for everything that happens to us.

I think of God as the constant companion who is every bit as sad as we are when we are treated badly. In other words, God is with us in times of great joy *and* in times of great sorrow. God is with us in times of great peace *and* in times of significant anxiety. God is with us in times of contentment *and* in times of great indignation. God is always with us, and God is always empathizing with us.

## Making Lemonade Out of Lemons

While God does not manipulate the circumstances of our lives to create in us the emotions he wants us to experience at any given moment; God is more than an empathetic bystander. Yes, God rejoices with us upon the birth of a child, a successful career move, and other such joyful occasions. God holds us and comforts us upon the death of a loved one or the loss of a career opportunity. However, God does even more. As part of God's loving covenant with us, God promises us that the Holy Spirit will be ever with us to offer us wise counsel, to help us recognize opportunities for further growth and development, and to satisfy our need for comfort and support.

To be sure, there is much we do not understand about the mind of God—how God works and doesn't work, or why things happen or do not happen. In the case of natural disasters such as hurricanes, earthquakes, tornadoes, and floods, the devastating effects cannot always be attributed to the free choices of any individual or group. Such circumstances serve to remind us that there are things, such as the laws of nature, that we cannot fully understand or control. However, even in the most difficult of those situations, God's love and mercy are with us. We are never abandoned.

## Practicing a New Paradigm

When we can imagine God as our best friend, biggest fan, constant companion, *and* the love of our lives, we can then fully engage a number of interesting and productive ways to nourish the relationship that we share. All aspects of our lives can be seen through the lens of this beautiful friendship. At that point, as we live life in the context of this deep and abiding friendship with God, our lives can become a continuous prayer. This realization opens us to the notion of seeing all that surrounds us and all that happens to us as opportunities for prayer.

In order to experience this new way of living, we accept that it is possible to live in this way; and then we develop the ability to consistently approach life accordingly. With God's help, we can then train our minds and our hearts to think and act in harmony with this new paradigm.

As with any skill that we hope to master, we will need to dedicate significant time and energy to practicing this new way of being.

## The Art of Reflection

Socrates embraced the principle that "the unexamined life is not worth living." Thousands of years later, this philosophy is still embraced by spiritual seekers of every faith tradition who fervently believe that we must take time to reflect upon our lives in order to get the maximum spiritual benefit from them. Every major event and decision that we encounter is an opportunity for new learning. And new learning leads to growth. From a spiritual perspective, growth means coming closer to God and to what God desires for us.

We have already noted that our current culture rewards activity, speed, and immediate gratification. These attributes fly in the face of reflection, prayer, and patient discernment. More than thirty years ago, Jesuit theologian Karl Rahner emphatically proclaimed: "The Christian of the twenty-first century will be a mystic or will cease to exist." Rahner was predicting that, if we don't find time in our busy schedules for quiet moments of companioning with and listening to God, we will most certainly lose our bearing and literally abandon our sense of the sacred. It has often been said that Christianity is countercultural because it espouses principles of peace, love, mercy, and "turning the other cheek." It is also countercultural because it endorses patience, quiet, solitude, and reflection upon the sacred. Moreover, it encourages emptying the mind (via the activity of contemplative prayer) as opposed to filling the mind with constant stimulation and the bombardment of the senses.

Both silent reflection and contemplative prayer (quieting the mind) provide opportunities to find sacred balance in our lives. As catechists, we do well to practice these forms of prayer, which enable us to calm and center ourselves. As we grow in our ability to accept the peace that only Christ can give, we become models of that peace for our students (and for their parents)—witnesses to the power of God to help us grow in peace, faith, and love. The choice is ours, to practice or not to practice this new paradigm.

### Approaching God in Prayer

A healthy detachment from our personal egos and our personal desires is key to a meaningful prayer experience. Moreover, we have a powerful message to that effect in the form of the prayer that was given to us by the greatest "person of prayer" who ever lived, Jesus Christ. It is The Lord's Prayer. Let's spend a few moments reflecting upon it.

Our Father who art in heaven, hallowed be thy name;
*(Our Lord and our God, you are everything a parent should be, and more!
We honor you now and forever.)*

thy kingdom come,
*(We pray for your reign on earth to be advanced every day by virtue
of our cooperation with your will.)*

thy will be done
*(Lord, may our will correspond to your will, and when that is not immediately
the case, may we grow to embrace your will over our own.)*

on earth as it is in heaven.
*(Heaven and earth are yours, O Lord. May we use our gifts and talents
to help bring about your glorious reign here on earth.)*

Give us this day our daily bread,
*(We pray that you will give us all that we truly need in order to live
a physically, psychologically, and spiritually healthy life.)*

and forgive us our trespasses, as we forgive those who trespass
against us;
*(We realize that forgiveness is key for a healthy life. In order to be in right
relationship with you, we must first be in right relationship with our neighbor.
We therefore commit to seeking and granting forgiveness.)*

and lead us not into temptation, but deliver us from evil.
*(Lord, we acknowledge the presence and power of evil in this world, and we ask
you to help us make good choices that will protect us from the damage that such
evil can bring to our relationship with you.)*

Amen.
*(So be it, dear Lord.)*

The Lord's Prayer has a number of very important constitutive elements. We are called to love and praise God as our sacred parent. We are instructed to help build the kingdom of God that is here but not yet complete. We are asked to surrender our egos, our wills, and all our concerns to the Lord. We know we have needs that only God can supply; therefore, we ask him, from his heart of mercy and love, to supply those needs. In order for God's kingdom to be completely realized, we must learn to forgive, just as God forgives us. We ask for God's constant assistance and protection. This is our profound prayer to the Lord.

God's love and mercy can penetrate every aspect of our lives, if we are willing to continue to build our relationship with God through the power of prayer. The choice is ours!

While I don't think of God as the master puppeteer, I do believe that he is active in our lives. God is always providing us with opportunities to grow and to experience joy; however, we have to meet him halfway. We must be open to new possibilities when they occur. We must be willing to act as co-creators, using the gifts, talents, and opportunities that God provides for us. And when we get knocked down, we must be willing to get up again—moving forward in faith and hope, embracing the love God has for us, and seeking and finding ways to respond in love. We are called to live our lives from the perspective of love, not of fear. Remember, "love drives out fear" (1 John 4:18).

## FOR REFLECTION AND DISCUSSION

- In your role as a catechist, have you ever found yourself asking: "Why did God put me through this?" or "Why did God allow this to happen to me?" Can you imagine that perhaps God was in the midst of your suffering, suffering with you and offering love and wisdom to help guide you through that difficult time? Write the story in your journal and reflect upon it. Share the story with another person when circumstances allow. If time allows, repeat this exercise by changing your role to that of a spouse, a parent, an employee, etc.

- In your journal, write the words of the Our Father. Write down one line at a time and leave space between each line. Meditate on what each line could mean to you in your role as a catechist. Which line(s) of the Our Father are the most powerful for you, and why?

- Have you ever made a decision based primarily on fear and upon further consideration realized you might have made a different decision if you had been considering love as your primary motivation?

- Search YouTube for versions of the Our Father that are set to music. Do any of these speak to your spirit in a profound way?

**PRAYING WITH SCRIPTURE**

MATTHEW 6: 9–13  •  1 JOHN 4:16–19  •  EPHESIANS 5:14–20

**PRAYING WITH MUSIC** *(available on YouTube)*

**"Love Broke Through"** | *Toby Mac*
(WWW.YOUTUBE.COM/WATCH?V=44L9PRI4C2M)

**"Here I Am, Lord"** | *Dan Schutte*
(WWW.YOUTUBE.COM/WATCH?V=ZBG-YDHM2KY)

**"Do Something"** | *Matthew West*
(WWW.YOUTUBE.COM/WATCH?V=B_RJNDG0IX8)

# CHAPTER FIVE

# The Stories of Our Lives

Each of us has stories to tell—stories about the people we've met, the places we've seen, the things we've experienced, and the lessons we've learned. Collectively, these vignettes form the story of our lives. Just as the characteristics of our minds and bodies are represented by our DNA, many of the details of our lives are represented by the stories we tell. To the degree that we reflect upon our individual stories, we learn more about who we are and why we do the things we do. Spending time with our stories is vitally important.

Scripture is *full* of stories, every one meant to help us know more about our salvation history. And the stories we read about Jesus in the gospels are particularly important for teaching us how to live as missionary disciples of Christ. In fact, the parables, stories that Jesus uses as particular teaching tools, are among the most powerful stories of all. Together, the stories in the Bible form the narrative of what theologians (and at least one Hollywood producer—George Stevens) have called "The greatest story ever told."

As catechists, it is important to recognize the incredible teaching power of stories. Dr. David Walsh, an internationally known psychologist and author, is fond of saying: "Whoever tells the stories defines the culture." When various stories compete for the attention of the general population, disagreements often arise and divisions can occur. For example, contemporary marketing agencies spend millions of dollars trying to convince us that the product they represent will make us truly happy. However, the stories of our faith tradition assure us that true happiness is only found in a loving relationship with the Lord. One thing we might all agree upon is that stories are teaching tools, and that a compelling story is a *great* teaching tool.

Link this with the theological principle of "situational spirituality" (everything we experience can be grist for further developing our relationship with God) and we have an important technique of good pedagogy. As catechists, we begin by naming and becoming comfortable with the stories that have shaped us. We then assist our students in recognizing and sharing their own stories. This helps them to make connections between their stories and the greatest story ever told. Good story listening and good storytelling are essential elements of quality catechesis.

In his book *It Was on Fire When I Lay Down on It*, Robert Fulghum illustrates the power of storytelling. One particular story takes place on the island of Crete where Fulghum attended a conference on Greek culture. The conference center was founded by an internationally known humanitarian named Alexander Papaderos who was devoted to reconciliation and peace between peoples and nations. Papaderos had grown up during World War II and knew of the fierce battles between Cretan residents and German soldiers. A childhood experience during the war shaped his life forever.

On the last day of the conference Fulghum asked Papaderos, "What is the meaning of life?" Here is the answer he received.

Taking his wallet out of his hip pocket, he [Papaderos] fished into a leather billfold and brought out a very small round mirror, about the size of a quarter. And what he said went like this:

"When I was a small child, during the war, we were poor and we lived in a remote village. One day, on the road, I found the broken pieces of a mirror. A German motorcycle had been wrecked in that place.

"I tried to find all the pieces and put them together, but it was not possible, so I kept only the largest piece. This one. And by scratching it on a stone I made it round. I began to play with it as a toy and became fascinated by the fact that I could reflect light into dark places where the sun would never shine—in deep holes and crevices and dark closets. It became a game for me to get light into the most inaccessible places I could find.

"I kept the little mirror, and as I went about my growing up, I would take it out in the idle moments and continue the challenge of the game. As I became a man, I grew to understand that this was not just a child's game but a metaphor for what I might do with my life. I came to understand that I am not the light or the source of light. But light—truth, understanding, knowledge—is there, and it will only shine in many dark places if I reflect it.

"I am a fragment of a mirror whose design and shape I do not know. Nevertheless, with what I have I can reflect light into the dark places of the world—into the black places in the hearts of men—and change some things in some people. Perhaps others may see and do likewise. This is what I am about. This is the meaning of my life."

And then he took his small mirror and, holding it carefully, caught the bright rays of daylight streaming through the window and reflected them onto my face and onto my hands folded on the desk.

Much of what I experienced in the way of information about Greek culture and history that summer is gone from memory. But in the wallet of my mind I carry a small round mirror still.   » pp. 175–77

I often use this story when facilitating retreats for catechists and other spiritual seekers. It serves as a gateway into profound introspection and conversation about the meaning of life; it is also an example of how personal stories and metaphors can unpack deep spiritual truths. What are the various ways you as a catechist can be a reflector of the light?

## Recording and Engaging a Story

Stories are only as effective as we allow them to be. Once we acknowledge that a story has power to shape us, we must then spend time reflecting upon it. We do this by asking ourselves questions. This is the act and the art of processing/engaging the story. And processing a story is truly an art, one that each of us can cultivate. As we engage with our stories, we become better at recognizing their significance and verbalizing those insights to other people who can benefit from our newly found wisdom. In doing so, we knit the fabric of relationships with other people and ultimately with God. And there we are again, right back to the importance of building relationships, the life blood of a life well lived.

Before we can properly process one of our own stories with someone else, we should begin to process it in prayer with our Lord. A good tool for initiating and recording this activity is journaling. In our fast-paced world, where much of our communication is defined by the limited number of characters of a tweet or a text, journaling goes against the flow of our busy lives. Even so, I implore you to "swim against the tide." The art of journaling is important for several very practical and spiritual reasons:

- it provides a logical sequential pathway for documenting the story;
- it gives us a location to store our thoughts;
- it provides an intimate setting, a comfort zone, which allows us to enter more deeply into the experience;
- it slows us down, enabling us to reflect more intentionally on the material we are processing.

This last point is one of the most important reasons for journaling. It takes time to write something on a piece of paper, more time than it takes to actually have a thought. Writing our thoughts allows us to spend more time with each one. This, in turn, gives us more time to process, leads to additional insight, and raises important questions. Journaling is time well spent; it enriches our prayer time, thus enhancing our relationship with the Lord.

I find one journaling technique to be particularly helpful. I begin every journal entry, as I might begin a letter (or an email), with the words: "Dearest Friend." Starting each entry with this or a similar salutation adds a level of intimacy. Moreover, the act of writing provides an opportunity to understand how God might be reacting to what I am writing. Thus, the letter becomes a two-way conversation, not merely a list of what I am thinking and feeling.

In the process of journaling, I often find the questions of my heart beginning to be answered by the Lord. At the very least, I find guidance regarding how I might refine the question or how I might act in order to move the concerns of my heart to the next stage of development. And, in case I ever forget the lessons I am learning during this time of reflection, I have them recorded in print and can return to them whenever I wish.

A close friend of mine has developed a wonderful habit of visiting both the present and the past with his journaling. Each night before going to sleep he writes in his journal. When he is finished, he reaches over to his nightstand and picks up his journal from the year gone by. He takes a few moments to read and reflect upon his entry from the same date during the previous year. This gives him added context for his spiritual journey, as he recalls what occupied his prayers exactly one year earlier and how those things have resolved, changed, or stayed the same. It is a beautiful prayer technique! If those you catechize are old enough to write, they are old enough to journal. Journaling is a wonderful spiritual tool for just about anyone.

**Personal Stories: A Foundational Element
in the Catechetical Process**
Several decades ago, Dr. Thomas Groome developed a catechetical process named "shared Christian praxis," which became a hallmark of his career as an educator and a master catechist. The basis for Groome's praxis correlates precisely with situational spirituality. That is, our lives provide the material (the stories) that we then hold up to the great story (the story of God's love for us, found in Scripture and the history/tradition of our faith). Groome writes that shared Christian praxis "calls for a real integration, so that the faith people profess and the lives they lead become, by God's grace,

integrated in their heads, hearts and hands. The 'learning outcome' of this approach is that Catholic Christian faith might become the core commitment of their lives, the identity by which they live" (Groome, *Compass*, p. 2 of 9).

Shared Christian praxis includes five stages or "movements":

1. *Naming:* This is the time for telling *the story* of what happened, including as many details as possible. For example, it could be the story of a fight between two children that erupted on the playground at school.
2. *Reflecting critically:* Delve more deeply into the situation using questions such as: Why did the fight occur? What led up to the fight? What were the participants thinking and feeling during the fight?
3. *Accessing the Christian tradition:* What do Scripture, tradition, and the teachings of the church tell us about ways to settle disputes?
4. *Integrating:* Students/participants reflect on their own understandings, experience, views, and questions in light of what they are learning about the larger Christian story and vision. This dialogue between their own story and the Christian story helps them deepen their understanding. This is a vitally important part of the process where true integrative learning occurs.
5. *Responding:* What are the participants being called to do? How are they being called to act in a manner that promotes peace as opposed to violence, based upon their learning? (Groome— *Christian Religious Education: Sharing Our Story and Vision*)

This technique of comparing and contrasting our own experiences (our stories) with the great story of Christian practice is an extremely valuable tool in the process of moral decision making. And its application is even more encompassing than that. Shared Christian praxis can be applied to any aspect of our faith development, using the stories of our lives. For example, at the moment when we are awestruck by a beautiful landscape or a heroic act of courage, we can apply the same process in order to come to know, at a deeper level, how God is acting in our lives in that moment. It is a wonderful process for encouraging growth and, when necessary, resolving conflict in many and varied situations.

## Stories: The Molecules of a Life Well Lived

Fred Rogers, a Presbyterian minister and the "Mr. Rogers" of PBS television fame, carried in his wallet a quote from a social worker: "Frankly, there isn't anyone you couldn't learn to love once you've heard their story."

The stories of our lives summarize who we are. And when these stories include connections with and reflections upon the stories of our faith, found in Scripture and the traditions of our church, we have the material for a wonderful tapestry of a life well lived as disciples of Christ—loving and being loved in a fashion that gives vibrant detail and meaning to the story of our eternal life, our eternal love affair with our very wonderful God!

## FOR REFLECTION AND DISCUSSION

- Recall a particular story (or two) that has played a significant role in your faith development. Share it with a friend.

- Write about this story in your prayer journal, including as many details as possible. Take time to reflect upon the story, paying particular attention to the emotions it evokes in you.

## PRAYING WITH SCRIPTURE

MATTHEW 13:10–13 • LUKE 10:29–37 • JOHN 6:1–15

## PRAYING WITH MUSIC *(available on YouTube)*

**"Eye Has Not Seen"** | *Marty Haugen*
(WWW.YOUTUBE.COM/WATCH?V=7JYGOQC82AU)

**"Lifesong"** | *Casting Crowns*
(WWW.YOUTUBE.COM/WATCH?V=G0JEEF9VB5M)

**"Better than a Hallelujah"** | *Amy Grant*
(WWW.YOUTUBE.COM/WATCH?V=RM5KX3XQMG0)

**"My Story"** | *Big Daddy Weave*
(WWW.YOUTUBE.COM/WATCH?V=1TKAN-NASU8)

CHAPTER SIX

# A Dynamic Duo:
# Trust and Surrender

Marie was a lovely twenty-seven-year-old woman from San Francisco. Her most notable features were her infectious joy, as represented by a smile that could light up a room, and her deep, abiding faith, a faith she was eager to share with anyone interested in hearing about it.

After graduating from college with a degree in education, Marie decided to spend time serving those in need. She joined the Volunteers in Service to America (VISTA), a sister organization to the Peace Corps. After a year and a half of VISTA service, Marie joined a contemporary Christian theater company, headquartered in a suburb of Los Angeles. There she met a single young man named Blain, who had similar aspirations of bringing others closer to Christ through drama. They corresponded, primarily through letters as they traveled in separate groups across the United States and Europe, performing for churches and other Christian organizations. After about a year and a half of this long-distance friendship, they were assigned to the same troupe traveling in Kentucky and Tennessee. During that four-month tour, they fell in love. But there was a "catch." Blain was discerning a call to the priesthood. As a Roman Catholic, this would mean saying no to marriage.

Marie knew that she loved Blain, but all she could do was wait. As she prayed for him and for their relationship, she felt conflicted. Was what she wanted what God wanted? If they did marry, would she be taking a potential priest away from the church? Her life, especially her prayer life, was in turmoil. Only one prayer seemed to give her the least bit of comfort. It was the prayer of surrender, the prayer that says to God: "Your will be done."

The prayer of surrender is perhaps the hardest one to pray. In doing so, you give God all control over your circumstances and agree not to manipulate the outcome. You acknowledge that you do not have legitimate control over the situation at hand. Moreover, you are saying, "Lord, your will is more important to me than anything else—even more important than anything I may want to gain from this situation. Lord, I want to conform my will to your will, because I love you that much!"

One of the most difficult things about the prayer of surrender is maintaining that attitude. There is a temptation to fall back into the attitude saying: "I want what I want, and I want it now!" We have become accustomed to having a great deal of control over a great many things in our lives, and we have developed the bad habit of expecting instant gratification. When we are hungry, we want food, and we want it fast. When we are sick or in pain, we want relief, and we want it immediately. When we are unsure about the future, we want answers and we wanted them yesterday! Generally, we expect to control the various aspects of our lives and to get what we want when we want it.

This tendency to expect immediate gratification flies in the face of a spirituality that embraces the premise that God is our creator, redeemer, and sustainer. God is the giver of all good gifts, including the gifts of life, love, and all of creation. Every moment of life is a gift from God. Every breath we take is the graceful Spirit of God at work in us. When we view our lives through the lens of giftedness, we become more appreciative of the many blessings God bestows upon us. This notion fuels an attitude of gratitude.

The attitude of gratitude is a key concept in any healthy spirituality. As mentioned earlier, Meister Eckhart taught that gratitude is the very foundation of prayer. This goes hand in hand with the prayer of surrender. When we can savor everything we enjoy, including life itself, as a gift from God, then we can appreciate how God is constantly working to bring goodness, mercy, and wholeness to our lives. Moreover, all that we are given by God, every gift and blessing, is given freely. Not only are we able to choose how we will use these gifts, we can even choose whether or not to accept them at all.

Those choices form the essence of another of God's great gifts to us: free will. God gives us many gifts and talents, abilities that, when used for good purpose, can bring great exhilaration and fulfillment to our lives. It is our joyous challenge to discover those talents for ourselves and, once we discover them, to choose how we will develop and apply them in ways that will make the world a better place. In doing so, we will also experience the elation of letting our spirit soar, as we become co-creators with our wonderfully creative God.

How does this factor into the prayer of surrender? For the answer to that, we look back to the Book of Genesis and the account of the Garden of Eden. In this story, God blesses his glorious creatures, man and woman, with countless gifts. However, there is one thing that they are not permitted to enjoy as their own—the fruit of the Tree of the Knowledge of Good and Evil. God puts humans to the test, in order to discover whether or not they are willing to accept that God is God and they are not (Genesis 3). Even with everything they already have, they want more. They want it all! They want the same power that God has. They are not content to accept that there will always be some things that are not within their control, some circumstances they will not be able to change.

## A Beautiful Prayer of Surrender

This principle is at the heart of the Serenity Prayer, which is prayed at every meeting of Alcoholics Anonymous and all similar "Anonymous" support groups. This prayer is actually the first two stanzas of a six-stanza prayer reportedly written in 1926 by Reinhold Niebuhr, a Lutheran pastor and theologian:

*God, grant me the serenity to accept the things*
*    I cannot change,*
*Courage to change the things I can,*
*    and the wisdom to know the difference.*

It takes a great deal of trust in order to earnestly pray the Serenity Prayer. If prayed sincerely, we acknowledge that some things are out of our control. Three possible reasons for this come readily to mind. First, the circumstances may be under someone else's control. For example, in the aforementioned story, Blain's decision regarding the priesthood/marriage was actually between him and God. Because Marie and Blain were in love, she had an *impact* on the discernment process, but not *control* of the process. Second, something can be out of our control because of the laws of nature. This includes occurrences such as floods, earthquakes, illnesses, and the like. In such circumstances, our only recourse is to choose how we will react. In the case of a weather emergency, will we seek shelter? In case of an illness such as cancer, will we seek treatment? Third, sometimes the unexplainable happens. A tumor disappears without having undergone any treatment; or we experience an unmistakable urge to take a new route to work and just happen to be present when another car crashes and we are able to help save the life of the driver. Miraculous occurrences such as these are beyond our understanding and can serve to demonstrate that there are some things about God that we cannot fully comprehend. Such miraculous occurrences are elements of the grandeur and the mystery that are characteristics of God.

Many of us sometimes feel a strong desire to control a situation that is simply beyond our control. In such cases, a spiritually wise person will pray the Serenity Prayer, or something very similar. However, even when we think we have given the situation completely to God, we may find ourselves taking it back. We begin to worry about it again as though it were our situation to change or to fix, ours to control. We may do this because we *really* want a specific outcome that seems difficult or impossible to achieve without exercising our own influence. Returning to the story about Marie and Blain—over the several months that it took Blain to discern his calling, Marie often found herself taking back the situation she had given over to God.

I refer to this as the "yo-yo principle." When I was a child, I would throw the yo-yo from my hand as if I was giving up all control of it. Then I would snap the string and it would come flying back to my hand. As an adult, I often find myself doing something similar with issues that are troubling me. In prayer, I say that I am giving my anxiety and my concerns to God. However, in the next moment I pull them back to myself, as if to say: "God, I don't really trust the notion that I am being called to give you the concerns of my heart."

I venture to guess that all of us have succumbed to the temptation described in the "yo-yo principle" at one time or another. It is a very natural part of being human. However, if we desire to enter more deeply and completely into a loving relationship with God, we will learn to overcome the enticement this principle represents.

### The Stigma Associated with the Concept of Surrender

According to *Webster's New World College Dictionary (fourth ed.)*, the most common definition of surrender, and the one that is generally implied in a secular (non-spiritual) context, reads as follows: "to give up possession of or power over; yield to another on demand or compulsion." The spiritual definition of surrender is more closely represented by the second definition found in that dictionary: "to give up claim to; give over or yield, esp. voluntarily, as in favor of another."

There is a vitally important distinction between these two legitimate definitions of surrender. The first is used in adversarial situations such as contests, battles, and wars. It implies that one contestant feels overwhelmed and unable to claim ownership over something that was previously in their control. They are forced to cede, unwillingly, control of an object or a situation. They have lost the contest. The second definition, applied to the concept of spiritual surrender, simply means that one party recognizes the right and responsibility of the other party to decide the outcome of a particular situation. Franciscan Father Richard Rohr, writing in his daily meditation (1/19/2015), offered the following distinction between the two meanings of surrender:

> Spiritual Surrender is not giving up, which is the way
> we usually understand the term. [Spiritual] Surrender is
> entering the present moment and what is right in front of
> you, fully and without resistance or attempts at control. In

that sense, surrender is almost the exact opposite of giving
up. In fact, it is a "being given to."

When we exercise the art of surrendering our will to God, we do
not try to assert undue influence over a situation that is not ours
to control. Moreover, we are affirming that we trust God to handle
the situation and that, even if the result is not what we might have
chosen, we will accept it.

While the end result of surrender to an adversary is defeat, dis-
consolation, and sometimes even despair, the end result of true surrender to God is relief from anxiety and the joy of knowing that
one has put God first in the process of working out the details of a
given situation. Furthermore, when we surrender/give over a set of
circumstances to God, we are often given the ability to help resolve
the issue simply by acting in accord with opportunities that God
provides in order to work toward a resolution.

In Marie's case, once she was truly able to give her concerns
about the future over to God, she was no longer worried that she
would say or do something that would add pressure to the situation. She was able to allow her love and affection for God and for
Blain to shine through. In a curious yet marvelous way, she felt
closer to God and to Blain, perhaps because there were no longer
any strings attached to her relationships with them. Her willingness to allow the situation to unfold without trying to manipulate
the outcome actually proved that her love was pure and sacred.

### Union with God

Being able to surrender the concerns of our hearts and minds to
the Lord, concerns that are beyond our control, is an important
step in deepening our loving relationship with God. Rohr believes
that true spirituality is not about perfection or control but about

deepening this relationship. While God loves us unconditionally and is always inviting us to enter more deeply into this loving union, it is up to us to accept the invitation and act upon it. When we surrender to God's love, care, and mercy, we move significantly closer to the heart of God.

Spiritual surrender, even though it implies surrendering to God, can seem like risky business. A number of spiritual writers have likened it to entering a very dark night. In her book *When the Heart Waits*, Sue Monk Kidd advises that, rather than allowing ourselves to be overwhelmed by fear or anxiety, "what we need to remember is that we're carried in God's divine heart, even when we don't know it, even when God seems far away" (p. 149).

Scripture presents many wonderful examples of individuals who trusted God enough to surrender to God's will. These include Abraham, Job, Mary Magdalene, and Paul. And with her response to the angel Gabriel after learning that she was to be the mother of Jesus—"Behold, I am the handmaid of the Lord. May it be done to me according to your word" (Luke 1:38)—Mary gives a beautiful example of complete surrender. In that moment, her life was changed forever in ways that she could never have imagined. In another powerful example of spiritual surrender, Jesus, feeling extreme agony in the Garden of Gethsemane, said to the Father: "Father, if you are willing, take this cup away from me; still, not my will but yours be done" (Luke 22:42).

It is unlikely that we will ever be asked to surrender in such a dramatic and decisive fashion. But the opportunities for spiritual surrender are present in our lives every day. With these opportunities come temptations to do the opposite—to attempt to take control when it is not ours to take. Our egos want the chance to increase their prestige by demonstrating that we can do it all on our own, and that we alone know what is best, how to get that

great result, immediately. Just as it has been from the very beginning, we are sorely tempted to "eat the apple" that does not belong
to us. When those times come, we are called not to try to become
God but to give the situation to God and to work with God for a
godly resolution.

Marie and Blain have been married for nearly four decades now.
Both have spent most of their careers in service to the people of
God through the ministry of religious education. Thirty-nine years
ago, Marie traded her yo-yo for an offering bowl. She offered her
life and her will over to God and never looked back. And now,
more than ever, she and Blain and God are in love!

## FOR REFLECTION AND DISCUSSION

- Do you teach your students any specific prayers? In addition,
  consider teaching them the Serenity Prayer.

- Have you ever had trouble surrendering to God something
  that is not yours to control? Write that story in your journal.
  What did you learn from that experience?

- Consider your role as a catechist. Over which aspects of that
  role do you have some control? Which ones are out of your
  control? Are you comfortable in distinguishing the things
  that you can (and should) control from the things that are not
  under your control?

## PRAYING WITH SCRIPTURE

JEREMIAH 1:4–9  •  JEREMIAH 29:11–14  •  MATTHEW 7:25–33

LUKE 12:6–8  •  JAMES 1:5–6

## PRAYING WITH MUSIC *(available on YouTube)*

**"Amazing Grace"** | *John Newton and John Rees*

(WWW.YOUTUBE.COM/WATCH?V=HSCP5LG_ZNE)

**"Oceans"** | *Hillsong United*

(WWW.YOUTUBE.COM/WATCH?V=DY9NWE9_XZW)

**"Love Will Hold Us Together"** | *Matt Maher*

(WWW.YOUTUBE.COM/WATCH?V=GD4DFXMUY-8)

**"Be Not Afraid"** | *Bob Dufford*

(WWW.YOUTUBE.COM/WATCH?V=BLTUDBGJ8DG)

**"I Will Lift My Eyes"** | *Bebo Norman*

(WWW.YOUTUBE.COM/WATCH?V=KPB2JC5EFGO)

**"Blessings"** | *Laura Story*

(WWW.YOUTUBE.COM/WATCH?V=JKPEOPIK9XE)

# CHAPTER SEVEN

# Forgiveness

If you were to ask a dozen people to give you a list of the most important characteristics of a healthy spirituality, you would probably get twelve distinct lists. However, one characteristic that is likely to be found on each of those lists is forgiveness—both the desire to seek it and the desire to grant it.

**Forgiveness: Asked and Offered**

Because we are not divine but human, we have all experienced two distinct contexts regarding forgiveness. One is the need to ask forgiveness of someone whom we have offended. The other is the need to offer forgiveness to one who has offended us. Either of these contexts for forgiveness can often be situated within very difficult circumstances. Yet dealing with and learning from both situations is a necessary prerequisite for living a life in harmony with the message and the mission of Jesus Christ. Once we have managed to deal constructively (in a healthy manner) with the need for forgiveness in our own lives, we are better prepared to support others who are seeking the courage, wisdom, and compassion to forgive those who have offended them and/or to ask forgiveness of those they have offended.

Occasionally a situation in which both aspects of forgiveness are involved will present itself.

**Megan and Bridget**

Several years ago, when I was hosting a diocesan catechetical conference, Megan, a catechist, friend, and member of my parish, approached me with a troubled look on her face. "I have a hard time teaching my students about forgiveness," she said. She went on to describe what a difficult virtue it is to put into practice. "Sometimes, when I am teaching the principle, sharing what Jesus says about it and how he was willing to forgive even those who crucified him, I feel like a hypocrite." She then told me the following story.

Megan had a job as a shift supervisor for nurses at a local hospital. Over the years she worked hard to become an advocate for both the patients and the nurses under her supervision. Over a period of many months she felt that her section was being overlooked for upgrades to equipment and programs designed to make the rigors of nursing more manageable and more pastoral. Funding that she felt should be coming to her wing seemed to be going to Bridget, the nursing supervisor in a different part of the hospital. Correctly or incorrectly, it was Megan's perception that Bridget was favored by the head of nursing, who made decisions about training, funding, and programs. In her frustration, Megan made a derogatory comment to some of her nurses about Bridget. The comment got back to Bridget who wasted no time retaliating. She did so by starting a nasty rumor about Megan, based on what Megan insisted was unsubstantiated innuendo.

Now it was Megan's turn to be offended. While some of her friends chose not to believe the rumor about her, others were troubled and wondered if there might be some truth in it. Megan's integrity was called into question and she was devastated.

Many months went by and Megan and Bridget were unable to reconcile their differences. Megan grew tired of the feud and the energy it was taking from her life. Bridget was still furious at Megan for her actions and convinced that Megan was not worthy of forgiveness. Eventually both women retired from their jobs, without resolving the conflict.

Megan was stuck. She wanted to move on, both spiritually and emotionally. She had come to realize that some things were simply out of her control, but she felt she was being held captive by the situation. All aspects of her life were suffering, even her role as a catechist, because a significant part of her spiritual and psychological growth was frozen in time. This was her state of mind when she approached me at the conference.

### An Invitation from the Lord: Learning to Forgive

Forgiveness is one of the most difficult and complicated principles to teach and to practice. There are several reasons why this is so. For one thing, it goes against our instincts. When we are hurt, we tend to want to fight back, to "get even," to "settle the score." But Jesus says: "Be merciful, just as your Father is merciful….Forgive and you will be forgiven" (Luke 6:36–37). And when Peter asked the Lord how often he should be willing to forgive those who sin against him, Jesus said: "Not seven times but seventy-seven times" (Matthew 18:21–22).

Sometimes, forgiveness is difficult to practice because it calls for deep and candid introspection on our part. We must ask ourselves questions such as:

- How have I contributed to this rupture in relationship that is causing tension and pain?

- Am I willing to take responsibility for my own actions and to apologize for anything that helped create this difficult situation?
- Am I willing to admit that I have things to learn about the fragile but important nature of human relationships?
- Am I willing to act upon my learnings, thereby giving evidence of conversion/change of heart?
- Even if I am willing to forgive and willing to seek the forgiveness of the other person, can I accept that we might never be reconciled, because the other person may not be willing to forgive me or may not be willing to accept any culpability for the damage to our relationship?

These are tough questions, but they must be carefully considered: only if we are willing to answer "yes" to each one are we truly prepared to seek and to grant forgiveness.

In *Traits of a Healthy Spirituality*, Melannie Svoboda notes that forgiveness begins at home. This means that we must learn to forgive ourselves in order to be able to forgive others. She offers this quote from C.S. Lewis: "If God forgives us we must forgive ourselves. Otherwise it is almost like setting up ourselves as a higher tribunal than God." Until we can accept that God forgives us for any and all of our transgressions, we cannot begin to forgive ourselves, nor can we truly forgive another for offending us.

The ability to accept forgiveness as well as the ability to extend forgiveness are greatly impacted by our ability to accept love and to love another. This important concept takes us back to a foundational principle of Catholic Christianity upon which all other aspects are based: our belief that God loves us unconditionally and that nothing we can do, short of denying God and God's love for us, can block the flow of God's love and grace into our lives. Like the ability to love and to experience love, the ability to forgive and to experience forgiveness is a divine gift. It is one that frees us from what family counselor Earnie Larsen has called "a heavy stinking bag of resentment."

Joan Chittister, writing in *God's Tender Mercy: Reflections on Forgiveness*, describes the danger inherent in choosing not to embrace and practice this virtue. She posits that what we don't let go of via forgiveness will continue to harm us. It poisons the mind and hardens the heart like concrete. It does little or no direct harm to the one who has offended us but acts like acid eating away at our souls if we are the ones who cannot forgive.

Chittister reminds us that sometimes our inability to forgive is linked to an unwillingness to put ourselves in the shoes of the person who has offended us. Whether logical or illogical, justified or unjustified, the actions of the offender are based on some type of reasoning. Moreover, those actions are also conditioned by what the offender has or has not learned about life, love, and mercy.

Moreover, she affirms the notion that to forgive someone is not to suggest that what they did to us was all right. It simply says that we are not going to let what they did destroy us.

## Megan's Forgiveness

When Megan first came to me with this problem, we agreed that a spiritual director might be able to help her sort it out and move forward. After hearing how long and how much Megan had been struggling with this situation, her director said: "Megan, you are putting a lot of psychological and spiritual energy into holding onto the hurt that you have felt at the hands of Bridget. You might want to consider how to deal with the parts of this story that you have some control over and how to surrender the remainder of the story and the resulting pain to God." Her director also spent time with Megan, discussing the many facets of forgiveness that we have examined in this chapter. Megan went away and prayed, considering all these things in her heart. When she returned for her next appointment she told her spiritual director that she was able to admit her own culpability. "It is not entirely Bridget's fault. I hate what she did to me, and I hate the fact that she has never made any attempt to apologize, but I can't control those things. What I can control is my own action. I think I need to write a letter to her sincerely apologizing for the hurt that I caused her."

Megan's spiritual director reminded her that she should not necessarily expect a reply to the letter. That was entirely up to Bridget. However, Megan could do two very important things in order to align her own spirit with the Spirit of God in this matter. First, she could write and send the sincere letter of apology and, second, she could pray to God for the grace necessary to release the anger in her heart in order to forgive Bridget.

To my knowledge, Megan has not received any response from Bridget. However, she has been able to forgive herself for the pain she caused and to forgive Bridget for lashing out at her. Equally important, Megan has felt a heavy load lifted from her shoulders and has a new spring in her step, especially when she walks into the room where she serves as a catechist. She enjoys teaching lessons on forgiveness, especially after the hard-won wisdom and freedom she has gained during her spiritual journey.

## FOR REFLECTION

[**NOTE:** *These questions are suggested for private reflection only. The responses may be too personal to share publicly.*]

• Can you name someone you have offended whom you have never asked for forgiveness? What makes it hard for you to ask that person for forgiveness? How might you prepare yourself in order to ask him or her to forgive you?

• Is there someone who has hurt you so severely that you have not been able to forgive them? What is holding you back from forgiving that person? What would help you prepare your soul and spirit so that you could forgive?

## PRAYING WITH SCRIPTURE

MATTHEW 6:14–15  •  MATTHEW 18:21–22  •  LUKE 6:27–42

LUKE 15:11–32

## PRAYING WITH MUSIC *(available on YouTube)*

**"Hosea"** | *Gregory Norbet, Mary David Callahan*
(WWW.YOUTUBE.COM/WATCH?V=I1NTIR3QGDY)

**"Forgiveness"** | *Matthew West*
(WWW.YOUTUBE.COM/WATCH?V=V8OHG8TUSSU)

**"The Hurt and the Healer"** | *Mercy Me*
(WWW.YOUTUBE.COM/WATCH?V=3XZAIVDBU9C)

**"Come as You Are"** | *Crowder*
(WWW.YOUTUBE.COM/WATCH?V=R2ZHF2MQEMI)

# CHAPTER EIGHT

# Dedicate, Dedicate, and Dance to the Music of God

When my father returned from his tour of duty with the U.S. Army at the end of World War II, he accepted an invitation from his older brother to join him as a partner in a small local hardware store. My father was blessed with a tremendous talent for doing mechanical things. He had a working knowledge of carpentry, plumbing, heating, electronics, etc. He also had great intellectual curiosity about how things worked and an ability to understand the answers to those questions. Dad lived his "calling" for many years and, as Scripture would say, he "grew and became strong, filled with wisdom" (Luke 2:40). Every day he would wake up and, in his own way, rededicate himself to the principles that made him a successful businessman as well as a wonderful husband and father. He lived each day with a sense of integrity, fairness, empathy, professionalism, and most importantly, faith. One of my favorite stories, gleaned from my father's thirty-five-year career as a hardware store owner, helps me understand how much I learned from him.

One day a bright young man named Tom, who had recently married and started a family, came into the store with a huge list of plumbing supplies that he needed for a major remodeling project for his modest home. Dad spent nearly an hour with Tom, helping him figure out exactly what he would need and how all the pieces would fit together in order to do the job properly. Tom had many questions, and Dad had the answers. My father was relying on his experience as a plumber, gleaned over many years of following his call.

As Dad was preparing to ring up the rather sizable sale, his curiosity got the better of him, and he said to Tom: "I'm curious about why you came to my small store to purchase these things. I know that you work in a large discount store that carries most of this. Because that store buys in huge quantities and because you work there and receive an employee discount, you could have purchased all this at a huge saving." Almost without hesitation, Tom said: "Mr. Miller, it's true that I could have purchased all of this very cheaply at that store. However, there is no one there that I trust to show me exactly what to do with it once I get it home. You not only showed me exactly what I need, but you took me through every step of the assembly process. Now I can go home and do this myself. You saved me the money I would have paid a plumber, and when I'm done I will feel really good about what I've accomplished."

Over the years I have regaled people with stories demonstrating the incredible gift my father possessed for working with his hands. However, it was only recently that I realized that one of Dad's greatest gifts was his ability to teach. Because he knew his profession so well, was excited about it, and loved to help people, he was always teaching others about some aspect of it. Even in casual conversations with others—on the golf course, in the grocery store, at a restaurant—Dad helped people solve their mechanical problems. It all came naturally to him, and all whom he helped were very grateful. Over the years, I learned some valuable mechanical lessons from my father; but, more important, I learned numerous significant life lessons as well. He was always teaching me something just by the way he lived.

By virtue of our baptism, we are commissioned to demonstrate the love of God to those we encounter, showing them how it forms us, sustains us, and propels us forward in life. Dad lived his baptism! When I do a workshop on catechesis I often remind catechists that we are always catechizing inside AND outside the classroom. The more we recognize this, the more likely we are to give witness to the loving relationship we share with Jesus Christ. We have dedicated our lives to building the Reign of God. Our success in doing so can only be measured by how well we give witness with our actions to that which we proclaim with our words.

### Dedicate and Rededicate in order to Rejuvenate

*Webster's New World College Dictionary (fourth ed.)* defines "dedicate" as "to set apart for worship of a deity or devote to a sacred purpose." What a wonderful definition to use when considering our roles as catechists.

In *Four Steps to Spiritual Freedom*, Thomas Ryan titles Step Four: "Daily Rededicate Your Life to God." He writes not only a rationale for the act of rededication, but a process we can use in order to write our own prayers of rededication. Since reading the book over a decade ago, I have found numerous applications for his helpful suggestions within my own life, with none being more practical or more helpful than Step Four.

Ryan's concept for the construction of the prayer—a prayer that should be uniquely tailored by and for each one of us—is based on the premise that, at the deepest level of our spirit, rededication is a willingness to surrender all to God.

For Ryan, daily rededicating our lives to God means constantly asking how we can best use our time, talent, and treasure to love and serve God. The act of rededication is a loving response to a God who is always inviting us deeper into relationship. It is an opportunity to fall in love with God anew each day.

Every morning I recite my very own prayer of rededication to our Lord. This is one of the most important things I do in any given day. This simple prayer, which I have constructed in my own words, sets the tone for the day by reminding me that I am dedicating my day as well as my very being to the One who gave me life—the One who loves me eternally, immeasurably, and unconditionally. After many years of saying my rededication prayer faithfully, it comes automatically to mind each day. In fact, my day is not complete without it.

As a diocesan director for catechesis, I sometimes found myself dealing with controversial issues. One day, while waiting for a return phone call from someone who was upset about an important policy that we were implementing, I took a moment to reflect upon my prayer of rededication. When the call came, I calmly and quietly reminded myself that my words and actions were dedicated to God and that God was with me. Although the caller and I were never able to come to total agreement, by God's grace we were able to come to a place of understanding and respect. In that situation and others like it, I have learned many valuable lessons about wisdom, integrity, courage, and the faithfulness of God. And, dear Lord, how I have grown! Moreover, my prayer of rededication has been a powerful tool for facilitating that growth.

## The Alpha and the Omega

In Chapter Three I wrote about the Examen. While praying the Examen is a great way to end a day, the prayer of rededication is a great way to begin it. And everything in between is a combination of various forms of being and acting that compose what we might call "the way we spend our waking hours." In this paradigm, rededication (at the beginning) and the Examen (at the end) form the bookends of the day.

I believe we are called to rededicate each day of our lives to God and to spend our energy throughout each day for him, pacing ourselves as we take ample time to rest in the Lord as well. And at the end of the day, as we reflect upon the many ways that God has been active in our lives and in the world that day, we once again have the opportunity to celebrate our love affair with our Lord!

## Catechists for All Time

Many years after my father retired and sold the hardware store, I asked him if he was disappointed that I did not succeed him in the business. In his own gentle way he said: "I didn't think you were that interested in the hardware business; I thought you would probably be a teacher." His answer was both wise and a bit ironic. In reality, he was one of the finest "hardware guys" as well as one of the best teachers I have ever had, even though he didn't officially consider himself a teacher. Only now do I realize that he and I are even more alike than I ever imagined. It causes me to smile—widely and warmly.

We are all catechists, all the time. We proclaim more about *our love for* and *our life with* Christ by what we do—both inside and outside the catechetical classroom—than by what we say, as important as our words are!

May your life, lived as a catechist—a missionary disciple of Christ—bring you great joy and fulfillment. May you give glory to

God in your words *and* in your actions. And may you always be *aware of* and *comforted by* the knowledge that God IS with you, God BLESSES you and God LOVES you like no one else ever can or will! Amen! Alleluia!

## FOR REFLECTION, DISCUSSION, AND ACTION

- Consider how the role of "constant catechist" plays out for you. What does your life say about your commitment to help build the reign of God now and for all eternity?

- Thinking back over your lifetime, who have been your favorite teachers? In what ways did they serve as catechists for you, either formally or informally?

- Pick one teacher from that list and write a prayer of thanksgiving to God about her or him. Share with God the things that have made that person so special in your life. Consider sharing these things with that teacher.

## PRAYING WITH SCRIPTURE

LUKE 2:22–33 • MATTHEW 6:19–21 • PHILIPPIANS 4:4–9

## PRAYING WITH MUSIC *(available on YouTube)*

**"Let Them See You in Me"** | *J.J. Weeks*
(WWW.YOUTUBE.COM/WATCH?V=KJHK39RVMQ8)

**"Glory and Praise to Our God"** | *Dan Schutte*
(WWW.YOUTUBE.COM/WATCH?V=C7GIWZG-AI4)

**"With Every Act of Love"** | *Jason Gray*
(WWW.YOUTUBE.COM/WATCH?V=V4BB7BUXBBY)

**"He Knows My Name"** | *Francesca Battistelli*
(WWW.YOUTUBE.COM/WATCH?V=1NHQJWDXFFE)

# BIBLIOGRAPHY

Anonymous. *How Can I Pray? (Daily Examen)*. Chicago: Loyola Press, ignatianspirituality.com, 2017.

Anonymous. *What Is Lectio Divina?* Rome, Italy: http://ocarm.org/en/content/lectio/what-lectio-divina, 2017.

Bacik, James. *Presentation Given to Catholic College and University Campus Ministers of the Catholic Conference of Ohio*. Columbus: 2005.

Chittister, Joan. *God's Tender Mercy: Reflections on Forgiveness*. New London, CT: Twenty-Third Publications, 2010.

D'Arcy, Paula. *Presentation Given at River's Edge Retreat and Conference Center*. Cleveland: 2015.

Fulghum, Robert. *It Was on Fire When I Lay Down on It*. New York: Villard Books/Random House, 1988.

Groome, Thomas H. *Christian Religious Education: Sharing Our Story and Vision*. San Francisco: Harper and Row Publishers, 1980.

—. *Bringing Life to Faith and Faith to Life: For a Shared Christian Approach and Against a Detractor*. Kensington, NSW: *Compass: A Review of Topical Theology*, Vol.40, #3, Spring, 2006.

—. *What Makes Us Catholic: Eight Gifts for Life*. New York: HarperOne, 2003.

Hays, Edward. *Chasing Joy: Musings on Life in a Bittersweet World*. Notre Dame: Peace Publishing/Ave Maria Press, 2007.

Keating, Charles J. *Who We Are Is How We Pray: Matching Personality and Spirituality*. Mystic, CT: Twenty-Third Publications, 1987.

Kidd, Sue Monk. *When the Heart Waits: Spiritual Direction for Life's Sacred Questions*. New York: HarperOne/HarperCollins, 1990.

Leonhardt, Douglas J., SJ. *Praying with Scripture*. Chicago: Loyola Press, ignatianspirituality.com, 2017.

Martin, James, SJ. *Between Heaven and Mirth: Why Joy, Humor and Laughter Are at the Heart of the Spiritual Life*. New York: HarperOne/HarperCollins Publishers, 2011.

Palmer, Parker. *Let Your Life Speak: Listening for the Voice of Vocation*. San Francisco: Jossey-Bass Publishers, 2000.

Pope Benedict XVI. *Caritas in Veritate* (Charity in Truth). Vatican City: Libreria Editrice Vaticana, 2009.

Pope Francis. *Evangelii Gaudium* (The Joy of the Gospel). Vatican City: Libreria Editrice Vaticana, 2013.

—. *Laudato Si'* (On Care for Our Common Home). Vatican City: Libreria Editrice Vaticana, 2015.

Pope Leo XIII. *Rerum Novarum* (Of New Things). Vatican City: Libreria Editrice Vaticana, 1891.

Rolheiser, Ronald. *Prayer: Our Deepest Longing*. Cincinnati: Franciscan Media, 2013.

Ryan, Thomas. *Four Steps to Spiritual Freedom*. New York/Mahwah: Paulist Press, 2003.

Saint Pope John Paul II. *Sollicitudo Rei Socialis* (The Social Concern of the Church). Vatican City: Libreria Editrice Vaticana, 1987.

Svoboda, Melannie. *Traits of a Healthy Spirituality*. Mystic, CT: Twenty-Third Publications, 1996.

United States Catholic Bishops. *Economic Justice for All*. Washington, DC: United States Conference of Catholic Bishops, 1986.

—. *Our Hearts Were Burning Within Us*. Washington, DC: United States Conference of Catholic Bishops, 1999.

—. *The Challenge of Peace: God's Promise and Our Response*. Washington, DC: United States Conference of Catholic Bishops, 1983.